Merry Christmas
love Annie
Joseph

To

....

From

....

Occasion

....

Date

....

Meet Me In the Garden

Pauline Ellis Cramer

Paintings by Katia Andreeva

HB
HONOR
BOOKS

Tulsa, Oklahoma

Meet Me in the Garden
ISBN 1-56292-816-3
Copyright © 2000 by Pauline Ellis Cramer
P.O. Box 50673
Idaho Falls, ID 83405-0673

Published by Honor Books
P. O. Box 55388
Tulsa, Oklahoma 74155

This book is dedicated
to my three friends
who prayed me through
the hardest year of my life –
the year my husband was killed.

GOD BLESS YOU.

Harriet Henderson

Marilyn Larson

Tiz Lum

This book is an open gate
inviting you to come inside
and witness how God changes a garden's beauty
through the four seasons.

Take my hand
and I will show you
some of the wonders of God's character
that He reveals through the rocks, roses, and oregano.

It is my prayer that your little visit with me in the garden
will bring peace to your soul
and encouragement to your heart.

Greenhouse Christians

Like newborn babies,

crave pure spiritual milk,

so that by it you may grow up

in your salvation.

1 PETER 2:2

Dear Lord, help me leave the greenhouse behind.
Grant me a mind that yearns for Your Word
and a heart that is brave enough
to step out of my comfort zone
and to risk growth.

I opened the door to my greenhouse only as far as necessary, and slipped inside, hoping the gust of cold air wouldn't traumatize my young plants. Shrugging off my coat, I surveyed rows and rows of delicate seedlings. Each one was my baby needing special attention. During their germination period, these seedlings enjoyed exact conditions for their birth. The pansies and parsley preferred darkness, but the celery and salvia called for light. Cucumbers not only needed the safety of the greenhouse but also extra warmth for their soil. I provided this with heating coils under their flat trays.

NOW THAT MY PLANT BABIES HAVE OPENED THEIR FIRST LEAVES, THE GREENHOUSE SHELTERS THEM FROM FROST AT NIGHT. FANS KEEP THE MIDDAY SUN FROM GENERATING TOO MUCH SOLAR HEAT. SPRING'S HEAVY RAINS NEVER TOUCH THEM. INSTEAD, I WATER THEM GENTLY FROM A FRENCH WATERING CAN. FED AND CARED FOR LIKE INFANTS, THEY THRIVE IN THIS SAFE GREENHOUSE WORLD.

Once my seedlings become strong, I'll move them outside to work for me. They will bring delight to me with their vegetables, herbs, and flowers. I will watch over them, water them when they are thirsty, and fertilize them when they are hungry. I will protect them from the evils of pests and weeds.

As they grow, they will be tested by thunderstorms, high winds, and scorching summer days. The work of growth and producing for me, however, is theirs to accomplish.

Becoming a Christian can be like birth in a greenhouse. The Holy Spirit plants the seed of faith within us and gently cares for it as it germinates. The Scriptures protect us with encouragement when we face the heat of opposition. Spiritually mature believers gently nurture our growth toward a stronger trust in Christ. Many of us, however, want to remain in our greenhouses. We demand that other believers continuously comfort us, that ministers spoon-feed us the Scriptures, and that elders rescue us from life's storms.

WHEN GERMINATION IS COMPLETED AND FAITH BEGINS TO GROW, IT'S TIME TO VENTURE OUT OF THE GREENHOUSE.

If we stay inside, we will become root-bound, simply struggling to remain alive. Our enthusiasm for spiritual growth will fade. Each time I say, "Okay, Lord, I'm going to do what Your Word says; I'll risk showing people Your love by my actions. (I'll teach some children, or I'll volunteer at the hospital, or I'll spend a morning at the soup kitchen.) I'm scared, but I'll trust You to guide me." That's when I step out of the greenhouse and begin to "grow up in my salvation."

Garden Garnish

I have found the following soil recipe the best to use for seedlings:

1 part vermiculite

1 part perlite

1 part sphagnum moss

smidgen of compost

2 teaspoons Soil Moist to one gallon of above mixture.

Only when I apply the Scripture
does God do the actual changing
in my thinking and my actions.
—EVELYN CHRISTENSON

When I consider your heavens,
the work of your fingers,
the moon and the stars,
which you have set in place,
what is man that you are mindful of him,
the son of man that you care for him?
You made him a little lower than the heavenly beings
and crowned him with glory and honor.
PSALM 8:3-5

Daffodil
Prophets

ONE EVENING I WATCHED A SHOW ON TV ABOUT THE MARVELS OF THE UNIVERSE. I HAD THOUGHT THAT THE SHOW WOULD GIVE ME MORE WAYS TO PRAISE GOD FOR HIS MAJESTIC CREATIVITY. INSTEAD, I LET IT STEAL MY JOY.

When the program concluded, I felt as if I were an insignificant grain of sand on the shores of space. David described my feelings when he penned the words of Psalm 8. I, too, wondered how a God who created the cosmos could possibly care about me and the small struggles of my life. The next morning, I wandered out to my spring garden to take comfort from my flowers. Four miniature white daffodils greeted me. With a disheartened sigh, I stared at the little daffies, hoping to absorb some of their cheerfulness. Their lovely heads bobbed up and down in a light breeze, and a flash of pale yellow captured my gaze. The center of some of them had a soft yellow tinge. I looked through the group and saw they opened with lemon yellow center cups that eventually turned a creamy white like the outer petals. As I looked closer, I noticed that the edges of the center cups were tiny scalloped ruffles.

The more mature blooms had pure white thread-like veins fanning through the petals, resembling fibers in the sheerest silk. These miniature spring trumpets, surrounded only by barren soil, were tiny prophets declaring the coming of God's glorious summer bounty. They displayed perfectly designed, minute beauty crafted by a majestic God. He creates and cares for not only macrocosms but also microcosms. God's intricate touch on those tiny flowers gave hope to my discouraged heart. He knew last fall that I would need their assurance. He gave life to the bulbs after I planted them. He gave hope to my troubled heart when He led me to find them in my garden. They told me one of the mysteries about God: He is not confined by time and space like you and I. His heart is big enough to love the stars and the daffodils. His heart is big enough to love you and me.

Thank you, Lord, for Your measureless love.

11

Garden Garnish

For centuries, daffodils have been among the most popular of garden flowers. Theirs is a spring ministry of relief and comfort to winter's starved souls.

They can bring delight in borders, rock gardens, containers, or almost any place you want a splash of color. They are hardy bulbs that must be planted in the fall. They are, however, touchy about drainage, so avoid low spots.

> He paints the lily of the field,
> Perfumes each lily bell;
> If He so loves the little flowers,
> I know He loves me well.
> —MARIA STRAUS

Battling Boulders

With the vision of six theme beds, I labored with the speed and strength that only a new garden project can propel. In a mere three days, I double-dug the beds for the Shakespearean, herb, fragrance, butterfly, and Bible plants.

The reality of my mini-motif garden seemed merely a shovelful of soil away.

I neared the final section of bed number six when my shovel made the sound all Rocky Mountain gardeners dread—the scrape of metal on rock. A few more experimental stabs in the earth with grating echoes, and I knew a sizable boulder lurked there.

But I gave them this command:
Obey me, and I will be your God and you will be my people.
Walk in all the ways I command you,
that it may go well with you.
But they did not listen or pay attention;
instead, they followed the stubborn inclinations of their evil hearts.
They went backward and not forward.
JEREMIAH 7:23-24

The next two days I dug, tugged, and toiled with my trowel, shovel, and pick mattock. It became more than mere rock removal. It was a battle of wills—mine against nature's. During one time of frenzied digging, I slammed down my shovel and yelled, "Don't you know God gave people dominion over the earth? Now give it up!" I stared at the boulder as angry tears cut white paths down my dirt-encrusted cheeks. Still focusing on the rock, I felt the weariness of battle flow down my arms and legs. I sank to my knees. Perhaps because I was kneeling, I turned to prayer. "Lord, will You help me outsmart this rock?" My eyes were still closed when a picture of a "B.C." cartoon formed in my mind. One of the little cavemen was lifting a boulder with a wedge and lever. A cartoon. God was speaking to me through a cartoon? What a sense of humor He has!

"Yes!" I yelled. Jumping to my feet, I raced off to borrow my husband's crowbar, then found a rock the perfect wedge size. I pushed with all my strength. The boulder came loose with a reluctant sucking sound. I pried the defeated stone over to a nearby gravel path then sat on it—savoring success. "Thanks God. I don't know why I didn't ask for Your help sooner. You've been gardening a lot longer than I." I don't know why I also forget to ask for God's help when I am trying to dislodge my soul's stones of stubbornness. I focus on the problem and forget to seek the solution. It's usually during my daily prayer times that God helps me change my focus. I still struggle at removing my stones of stubbornness, but when I ask for help, God comes to gently lever them away.

Lord, help me move forward in my faith
by listening and paying attention to Your will
instead of my own stubborn heart.

Garden Garnish

Theme beds or gardens offer an opportunity to focus your plant selection around a unifying idea. A theme that I've enjoyed planting is a Moonlight Garden. Every plant is white or silver, capturing the glow of the moon and stars. Some plants I've included are: silver lace, dusty miller, nicotiana (it is especially fragrant at night), white dreams petunias, rocket white snapdragons, iceberg roses, and baby's breath.

Men trip not on mountains,
they stumble on stones.
—INDIAN PROVERB

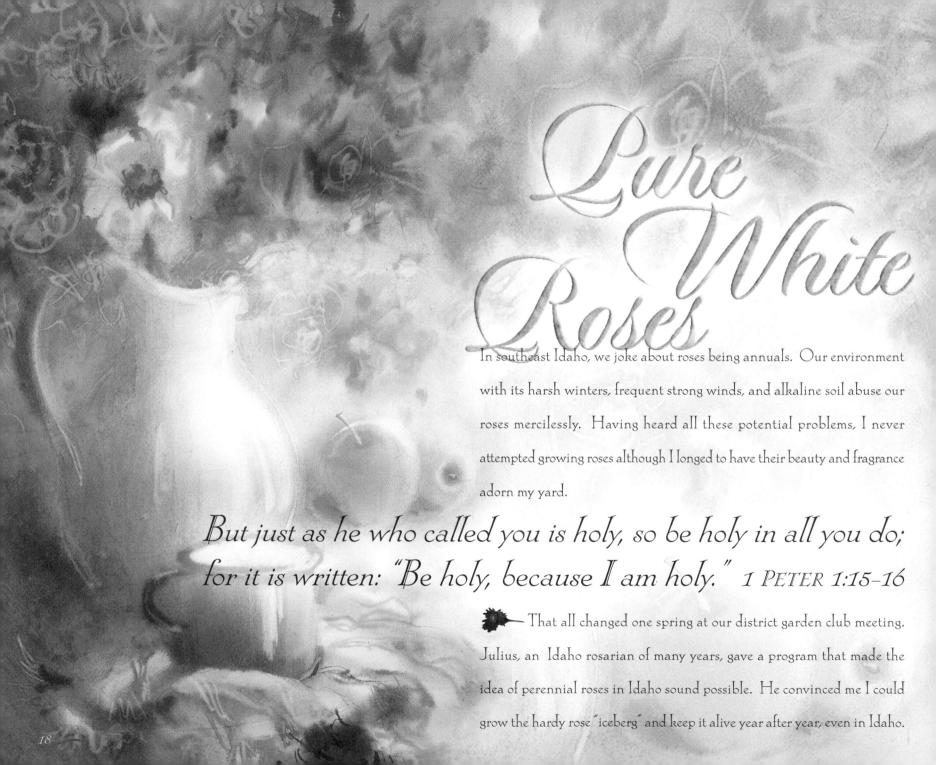

Pure White Roses

In southeast Idaho, we joke about roses being annuals. Our environment with its harsh winters, frequent strong winds, and alkaline soil abuse our roses mercilessly. Having heard all these potential problems, I never attempted growing roses although I longed to have their beauty and fragrance adorn my yard.

But just as he who called you is holy, so be holy in all you do; for it is written: "Be holy, because I am holy." 1 PETER 1:15-16

That all changed one spring at our district garden club meeting. Julius, an Idaho rosarian of many years, gave a program that made the idea of perennial roses in Idaho sound possible. He convinced me I could grow the hardy rose "iceberg" and keep it alive year after year, even in Idaho.

As soon as the ground thawed, I planted my bare-root iceberg rose exactly as Julius instructed. Then I nearly forgot about it as spring gardening duties demanded my full attention. One summer morning I stepped out our front door and glanced over at the flowerbed by the entry steps. Enthroned in the center of the rose bush was a single pure white rose with two buds on either side like guardian angels. I became instantly hypnotized by its luminous purity. "This is a hint of what God's holiness is like," my heart told me. The pristine petals glimmered and shined against the dark backdrop of our brown porch, creating for me a powerful image of God's glory in a world darkened by sin. My soul was drawn to that symbol of perfection as a person lost in darkness is drawn toward a light.

Our fallen natures, plus hostile environments, create sin within us that separates us from God's holiness. Through Jesus' sacrifice on the cross and His resurrection, a path is opened to us to be cleansed of our sins. When we confess our wickedness and trust in Jesus' sacrifice, we are given a new nature. We develop different priorities and interests than we had before and are set apart for God's use. Through obedience and a whole-hearted devotion to God, we are empowered by His Holy Spirit to overcome sin. The iceberg rose bush gave me a long profuse season of beauty. Every summer day until we moved, I kept at least one white rose in a vase on my desk. Throughout the day as I glanced at it, I became inspired by its purity. It continued to remind me of God's holiness and His call for me to imitate Him. With an uplifted spirit, I whispered David's prayer: "Create in me a pure heart, O God, and renew a steadfast spirit within me" (Psalm 51:10). *Heavenly Father, thank You for the power of Your Holy Spirit working to create a new, holy nature within all Your believers. Amen.*

Garden Garnish

Bare-root plants, including rose bushes, can save you 10 to 70 percent off the price of the same plant purchased in a container.

When you plant a bare-root, it has to grow in only one kind of soil. This helps the plant establish itself faster. For successful bare-root planting, soak the roots overnight in a bucket of water.

Place iceberg roses in full sun, with good air circulation, but sheltered from strong winds. The soil needs to be well-draining, well-dug, and compost-enriched.

It is quite true to say,
"I can't live a holy life,"
but you can decide to
let Jesus make you holy.
—OSWALD CHAMBERS

Come to me,
all you that are weary
and are carrying heavy burdens,
and I will give you rest.
Take my yoke upon you,
and learn from me;
for I am gentle and humble in heart,
and you will find rest for your souls.
For my yoke is easy,
and my burden is light.
MATTHEW 11:28–30 NRSV

Time to Touch the Thyme

Sweet Jesus,
thank You for herbal touchstones
that testify to Your genuine reality.

I approach life at hurricane speed. For days on end, I race against time until my body starts screaming, "Slow down, now!" If I don't listen, I pay the consequences. Mornings find me still tired after eight hours of sleep. I carry a throbbing headache all day long that no aspirin can relieve. I drop, spill, and break things, then snap at my husband. Finally, I comprehend the message that I'm not accomplishing anything. In fact, I'm complicating my life. It's time to touch the thyme and rest in the Lord. I brew a cup of chamomile tea and inhale its sweet aroma as I carry it with me to the garden. My feet go directly to the section exclusively for herbs.

I BELIEVE HERBS ARE SPECIAL GIFTS FROM GOD THAT NOT ONLY ADD FLAVOR TO OUR FOOD AND HEALTH TO OUR BODIES, BUT ARE ALSO AVENUES FOR JESUS TO MAKE HIMSELF REAL TO US. HERBS SPEAK TO MY SOUL THROUGH ALL FIVE HUMAN SENSES. FOR ME, THEIR DELICATE FOLIAGE IN SOOTHING GREENS AND SILVER CREATE A VISUAL SIGNPOST OF JESUS' OFFER OF CALMING COMFORT.

I step past the oregano and sweet basil beds to run my hand over the thyme. Its pungent perfume reminds me of spaghetti dinners, pasta smothered in a rich red sauce shared with friends, and evenings filled with laughter and warm companionship. Jesus is saying to me that He is my friend and loves to give me human friends as channels of His love. Feathery dill leaves brush my arm, and I sense the gentle Spirit of my Savior's presence. I pinch off some parsley to freshen my mouth then sit on a bench to sip my tea and listen to the soft sound of butterflies dancing a ballet around the borage. Touching, tasting, seeing, and smelling these garden gifts makes my Savior seem almost tangible. I sit with Him and thank Him for this evidence of His love. He has promised the gift of eternal life with Him in the future, but these herbal presents offer signs of His loving friendship today. He is a brother that accompanies me now in the midst of a hectic world. The herbs tell me to "Rest for a few moments with Jesus. He will renew your peace and strengthen you to carry your yoke of responsibilities."

Garden Garnish

When you want to liven up a recipe with herbs but aren't sure which one to use, try thyme. It goes with a wide variety of meats and vegetables. It is a favorite of not only Italian cooks but is also used in many French dishes.

Common thyme is easy to grow. Fresh thyme is much preferred over the dried. I plant my thyme in close clumps that produce a quicker growing crop. Harvest the leaves before the flowers bloom. If you cut the plants to within two inches of the ground, it will give you another harvest before winter, even in a frigid Zone Four.

God's mercy was not increased when Jesus came to earth, it was illustrated!
—EUGENIA PRICE

Compost Confession

Suppose a brother or sister
   is without clothes and daily food.
If one of you says to him,
   "Go, I wish you well;
   keep warm and well fed,"
but does nothing about his physical needs,
   what good is it?

JAMES 2:15–16

WHILE WORKING ON MY MASTER GARDENER CERTIFICATION, I WAS REQUIRED TO ATTEND A THREE-HOUR CLASS EACH WEEK FOR FOUR MONTHS. I LOVED THE CLASSES AND LOOKED FORWARD TO EACH ONE. AT LEAST THAT WAS TRUE UNTIL THE WEEK CAME FOR THE CLASS ON COMPOSTING. I WANTED TO SKIP IT.

I carried a lot of guilt about composting. You see, I didn't do it, but no one knew my dirty little secret. All my gardening friends assumed that I composted regularly. Every gardener worth her seeds composts. Everyone, that is, but me. ———Yes, I knew composting was a superb way to recycle. I understood it would enrich my soil. I comprehended that my plants would wiggle their little roots through it while giggling with delight. I knew it was the right, responsible, resourceful thing to do. So, why wasn't I doing it?

The problem started several years ago when I asked my husband to help me build a bin for a compost pile. He forced my project into dormancy with three words: It'll draw mice." ———An occasional cat-face spider doesn't bother me. I'm not fond of snakes, but I let them go their way without panicking. Mice, however, turn me completely hysterical. The mere mention of rodents froze my whole body into non-composting paralysis. During the class on composting, the teacher raved about the benefits.

I sank lower and lower into my guilt. It was a relief when the teacher dimmed the lights for a slide presentation. ———At last—mercifully—the class ended. I fled the classroom and—literally—ran into one of my elderly classmates. ———On impulse I blurted out to her, "Clara, do you do composting?" She answered with confidence,

Dear God,
let all my actions be a witness
of my faith in You.

"I have a deep hole near my garden that I throw vegetation in, but no food. I worry about mice." I nearly hugged her as joyful relief flooded over me. I felt reprieved from my prison of guilt. 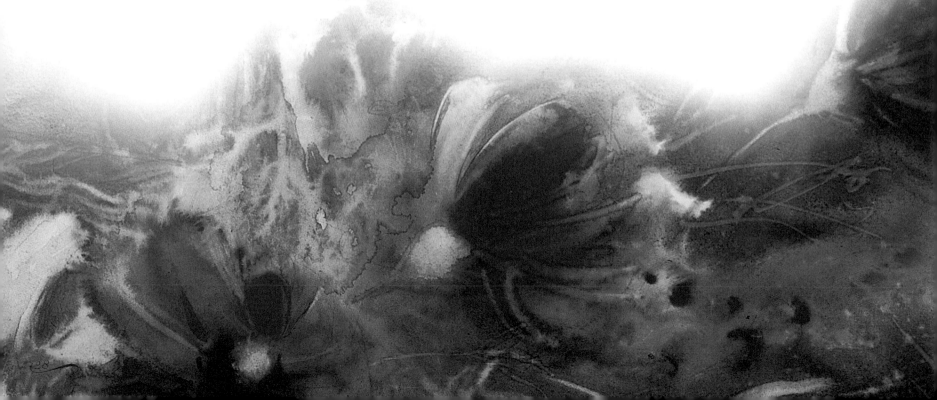 God gave me the answer to my problem through Clara. I knew that He timed my departure from the classroom perfectly. God cared enough for me to offer a simple solution. No, I didn't think my salvation was in jeopardy because I didn't compost. If my faith, however, is a dynamic part of all I do, then my actions need to result in good deeds. I could say, "I wish the best for this fair planet," then do nothing to care for it. As a believer, however, I was convicted because I knew composting was an opportunity for good stewardship of this earth. Each flower I feed, each tree I water, each plant I recycle nourishes the earth that God gives us to live on. Gardening responsibly is often hard work, but it can be an avenue for my faith to overflow into action.

28

Garden Garnish

To make the most efficient compost piles, alternate layers of vegetation with soil. Add grass clippings only in thin layers to prevent matting and smell.

Turn the pile once a week with a pitchfork and keep it moist. Compost is ready when it is a deep brown, crumbly, and has an earthy aroma—approximately after six to twelve months.

Earth provides enough to satisfy every man's need but not every man's greed.
—MOHANDAS K. GANDHI

29

Through God's Garden Gate

The last stop on our garden tour was Pat's home. The front of her residence resembled thousands of other suburban houses; that is, until we walked around the corner to a quaint garden gate.

Once we stepped through that gate,
we left the commonplace world far behind.

Our shoes crunched on pea gravel as we followed a path past catnip and lemon grass to a natural-looking arrangement of boulders. The sound of water trickling down the collection of sun-bleached rocks into a small pond invited us to rest on nearby limestone benches. Pat stooped beside the pool, disturbed the water with her fingertips, and made a kissing sound.

Do not be anxious about anything,
but in everything,
by prayer and petition,
with thanksgiving,
present your requests to God.
And the peace of God,
which transcends all understanding,
will guard your hearts and your minds
in Christ Jesus.

PHILIPPIANS 4:6–7

To our amazement, colorful coy fish surfaced through the water lilies to nibble the food she held in her hand. After discussing lily ponds and pet fish, the tour group moved on to another area of Pat's garden. I remained beside the pool, mesmerized by its tranquil beauty. Watching the orange, red, and gold coy glide through the water without worry or fear poured a flow of relaxation throughout my body. The serenely floating water lilies soothed away my anxious thoughts. Fast-paced schedules, difficult people, delays, and frustrations floated away on tiny ripples, leaving behind refreshment for my soul. Silently my heart overflowed with praise and thanksgiving to God for such a gift of peacefulness. The next morning as I studied my lengthy "to do" list, my heartbeat quickened as pressures and deadlines filled my mind. Then a flash of red from a passing car reminded me of the scarlet coy and the peace of Pat's water garden. *That must be similar to the peace God promises,* I thought, *but God's peace is even better because it's portable. I don't have to go sit by a water garden to find it; I can carry it with me wherever I go.* All believers can walk through God's garden gate at any time regardless of where we are. We have a standing invitation to deposit our stress outside the gate and enter His peace. He sets up a guard for our mind and heart that prevents the worries from entering the garden with us. For only a moment, or as long as we need, we can remain secure in God's garden, focusing our thoughts on His Son. Renewed by His presence, we can face this fallen world with the clarity of a worry-free mind and the confidence of a peace-filled heart.

Dear God,
Thank You for creating gardens
that guard our hearts and minds
as we face the brambles of everyday life.

Garden Garnish

Water gardens can be in anything from tubs just big enough to hold a single water lily to large ponds. You can create a balanced ecosystem with three ingredients:

(1) water lilies for replenishing oxygen and keeping the water cool;

(2) snails to eat algae and waste materials; and

(3) fish to eat pests such as aphids, flies, and mosquito larvae.

Cast all your anxiety on him because he cares for you.
1 PETER 5:7

Pumpkin-Vine Love

May the Lord make your love increase and overflow for each other and for everyone else, just as ours does for you.

1 THESSALONIANS 3:12

ONE FALL OUR GARDEN CLUBS HELD THEIR DISTRICT MEETING AT A BED AND BREAKFAST LOCATED IN THE MOUNTAINS NEAR OUR TOWN. AFTER A SUMPTUOUS LUNCH, WITH MUCH OF THE FOOD FROM THE OWNERS' GARDEN, THE WAITRESS ASKED IF WE WOULD BE INTERESTED IN TOURING THEIR HIGH-ALTITUDE GARDENS.

Barely able to contain our delight, we all followed the owner outside. To our amazement, we discovered an enormous pumpkin vine growing near one of their greenhouses. "I didn't realize you had enough frost-free days to grow pumpkins at this altitude," I said to the tour guide. He laughed. "We don't, but that's my secret." He pointed to an open window in his greenhouse. "I planted a few pumpkin seeds in the greenhouse and when the weather turned warm enough, I just opened that window. It did the rest, except that I occasionally added a little fertilizer to give it a boost." The pumpkin vine had climbed out the greenhouse window, slithered down the wall, meandered through a turnip bed, and then continued growing over a small chicken house. Although it was a crisp fall day, I believe it was still growing! That bountiful vine overflowing its source drew a picture for me of a true Christian. If we pray to be filled with Jesus' love for others, a miracle takes place within us. Love that is grounded in Christ overflows our hearts and reaches out to everyone. The writer of First Thessalonians prayed that the Lord would make our love increase for each other. We cannot produce such universal affection on our own, but when we root our love in God's power, it begins to grow with vitality. Nothing stopped that pumpkin vine—not windowsills, walls, or a hen house. If our love is grafted into God's strength, it can also climb past all human barriers. When we feel a lack of love for others, we can ask God for a growth booster from His endless supply. Then we need only look for opportunities to express that love in our homes and communities, over the next mountain or ocean, and even over a chicken coop.

Lord,
give me a pumpkin-vine love
rooted in You.

35

Garden Garnish

Pumpkins are a winter squash that varies in size from tiny jack-be-littles to giant prizewinner hybrids. We usually think of them as orange, but the cultivar lumina has white skin. Some nurseries label these white ones "baby boo."

When deciding which kind of pumpkin to grow, think of how you want to use it. Small sugar pumpkins make good pies, and jack-o'-lanterns are great for carving. If you want to win a blue ribbon for size, plant the prizewinner hybrid.

All pumpkins produce male and female flowers and can be hand-pollinated if the bees aren't buzzing. For extra-large pumpkins, allow only one female flower per plant to mature. Make sure the blossom has a good start before you pinch off the other female flowers.

Genuine Christian love . . .
is the one thing in the
Christian life which
cannot be
carried to excess.
—D. EDMOND HIEBERT

A Mismatched Love Affair

We have different gifts, according to the grace given us.
If a man's gift is prophesying,
let him use it in proportion to his faith.
If it is serving, let him serve;
if it is teaching, let him teach;
if it is encouraging, let him encourage;
if it is contributing to the needs of others,
let him give generously;
if it is leadership, let him govern diligently;
if it is showing mercy, let him do it cheerfully.

ROMANS 12:6–8

Heavenly Father,
help me learn what my gifts are
and grow them to glorify You.

It was a mismatched love affair from the beginning. It started one lonely winter day with the romantic book I bought about growing Victorian herbs, spices, and flavorings. Each page portrayed, in glowing color, picturesque herbal gardens. During each new snowstorm that winter, I escaped into the book to daydream over the captivating designs. With each falling snowflake, my passion grew for an enchanting herb garden of my very own. In the midst of a blizzard, I sent off my seed order. I was still a prisoner of infatuation when the seeds arrived.

AS I OPENED THE MAIL AND DISCOVERED THE SEED PACKETS, CHARMINGLY ILLUSTRATED WITH VICTORIAN MOTIFS, I ARRANGED THE SENTIMENTAL PICTURES LOVINGLY ACROSS OUR DINING ROOM TABLE. I SPENT HOURS DELIGHTING IN DESIGNING MY FANTASY GARDEN.

At one point I flipped over a package of sesame seeds to read the cultivation instructions: "... tender annual—native to the tropics." I naively dismissed the warning, having complete faith in the warm embrace of plastic walls-of-water for frost protection. My sesame seeds did germinate and struggled to grow. Our mild days and cool nights, however, stunted them to about one-third their normal size. Before they produced their purple flowers or seed capsules, our late August freeze turned them black. The same frost also destroyed my rosemary, cinnamon basil, and English lavender. The love affair was over. My dreams of a Victorian herb garden died with the frozen plants. It wasn't that my plants failed—they tried their best to grow—nor could I be accused of failing to care for them. I gave them more adoring attention than anything else in my garden. It was merely that few tropical plants survive in high altitude deserts.

I STOOD IN MY GARDEN LOOKING FIRST AT THE BLACKENED HERBS AND THEN AT MY ROBUST SNAPDRAGONS. "YOU FAILED AT HERBS," I TOLD MY BROKEN HEART, "BUT YOU GREW GREAT FLOWERS!"

That comparison was a graphic picture of human nature for me. Often we believe that if we can't grow Victorian herbs, sing like Pavarotti, paint like Thomas Kinkade, or make floral wreaths like our neighbor, then we are failures. God doesn't condemn us for not demonstrating skills He never gave us. He wants us to develop the gifts He blessed us with at birth. A failure in one area of our lives doesn't mean we are failures. It simply means we nurtured the wrong seeds. Whether we grow orchids or onions—preach to thousands or encourage one preschooler—our families, churches, and communities need our gifts.

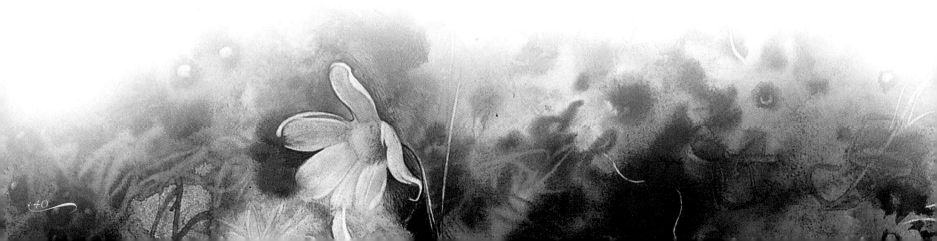

Garden Garnish

After my passion cooled and my logic returned, I researched herbs. I discovered many that grow well even in colder climates. Protected with mulch while getting established, these are good choices: Russian sage, chamomile, chives, dill, oregano, parsley, thyme, and mint.

Though a particular course of undertaking of yours failed, you are still a beautiful creation of God.

—STANLEY C. BALDWIN

January
Delight

The LORD your God is with you,
he is mighty to save.
He will take great delight in you,
he will quiet you with his love,
he will rejoice over you with singing.

ZEPHANIAH 3:17

FREEZING TEMPERATURES AND CLOUDY SKIES IN LATE JANUARY MADE CRAWLING OUT OF MY WARM BED ALMOST PAINFUL. SUNSHINE AND THE HOPE OF SPRING SEEMED A LIFETIME AWAY. WRAPPED IN MY WARMEST ROBE AND FUZZY SLIPPERS, I SHUFFLED TO THE KITCHEN. AS THE COFFEEMAKER GURGLED TO LIFE, I DRIFTED INTO

the living room to check for the bijillionth time the bulbs I was forcing. My fuzzy slippers slid to a stop when I glimpsed from across the room a hint of purple in the flowerpot soil. I flipped on the overhead light and rushed to my ceramic planter. There to my delight stood my first blooming crocus with its tiny plum petals just beginning to open. What joy that crocus brought to my heart! I had lovingly nurtured it for weeks and now it repaid me with its colorful appearance. It offered me a gift—the confidence that spring would arrive on schedule as usual, and I would get to indulge in my gardening delights once again.

A purple crocus wasn't all I discovered that morning. My eyes also found a seed of hope, a bright beauty in a bleak world, a reaffirmed promise from God. Although I don't have a singing voice—and my husband was still sleeping—my heart was singing. I no longer focused on the foot-high snow covering our patio. I no longer heard the north wind howling around the corner window. I simply sipped my coffee, gazed at the tender purple petals, and delighted in a God Who loved me enough to give me a winter gift. As I sat there in the quiet, I recalled a special verse, Zephaniah 3:17. It took on new meaning that cold January morning. Could God possibly "delight" in me as much as I delighted in my crocus? I have often been calmed by God's love, but does He "rejoice" over me with singing? How could something that incredible be true? I'm no one special—a wife, mother, and grandmother, nothing more. Yet, our majestic God delights in me!

I knew God loved me because He sent His only Son to die for me. But now a whole new aspect of that love opened to me. This verse belongs to all believers—even you and me. God is with us, saves us, delights in us, loves us, and rejoices over us as His precious children. Yes, He does sing with delight over us all.

Loving God,
I delight in knowing and serving you.

43

Garden Garnish

Crocuses are not true bulbs. They are corms, but I don't think they mind being called bulbs. They act like a bulb and need similar care. Corms are just stems that have become a storage unit. If you cut them in half crosswise, no rings are visible as in bulbs.

Crocuses are loved for being one of the first hardy flowers of spring. They show off their beauty best when planted in clumps or loose drifts. They add a special charm to woodland gardens, rock gardens, and, of course, containers.

The beauty of the world
is Christ's tender smile
coming to us through matter.
—SIMONE WEIL

All the world is an utterance of the Almighty.
Its countless beauties,
its exquisite adaptations,
all speak to you of Him.
PHILLIP BROOKS

About the Author

A certified Advanced Master Gardener,
Pauline Ellis Cramer
loves to help others discover the joys of gardening.

She also loves to write
and has published more than seventy articles,
stories, and devotionals.

She lives in Idaho Falls, Idaho,
where she enjoys trying new plant varieties in her greenhouse.
Her specialties are herbs and everlastings.

She has two children, Juddaca and Jim,
and three grandchildren, Maddie, Judd, and Lydia.

To contact the author:

Pauline Ellis Cramer

P. O. Box 50673

Idaho Falls, ID 83405-0673

pec1129@aol.com